1. **Introduction**

Understanding the adjustment mechanisms for prices and wages is crucial for understanding how monetary policy affects the economy. The broad consensus is that policy innovations have significant real effects, at least in the short run, because nominal prices and/or wages are not completely flexible. However, while a number of studies document the existence of sticky prices at the micro level (see Klenow and Malin (2010) for a summary), there is almost no direct empirical evidence on whether nominal rigidities—prices or wages—are in fact the primary reason why nominal disturbances such as monetary policy shocks affect real activity.

Olivei and Tenreyro (2007), use a VAR-based approach to assess the role of wage rigidities in monetary policy transmission. They show that the response of aggregate output to a monetary policy shock varies greatly depending on the shock's timing: A monetary policy shock that occurs in the first or second quarter of a given year has a sizeable effect on output that dies out relatively quickly, while a shock that occurs in the third or fourth quarter has very little effect on output. Olivei and Tenreyro argue that this result reflects the uneven staggering of wage adjustment. Anecdotal evidence on wage setting suggests that in the United States, a relatively large fraction of wage rates are re-contracted in the second half of the year.[1] Hence, if a monetary policy shock occurs in the latter half of the year, when wages are being reset, the shock will have a larger effect on labor costs and a smaller effect on output relative to a period in which wages tend to be more rigid. In addition to the findings on the time-dependent responses of output to monetary policy shocks, Olivei and Tenreyro find that prices respond with a delay when shocks occur in the first half of the year but respond quickly to shocks that occur in the second half of the year. They argue that these findings, along with the anecdotal evidence, indicate that uneven wage staggering plays an important role in the transmission of monetary policy shocks.

---

[1] The evidence on the timing of wage contracting that Olivei and Tenreyro (2007) discuss comes from the Federal Reserve's "Beige Book," the Radford Survey of compensation practices in the information technology sector, Bureau of Labor Statistics reports, and various other sources.

This paper uses disaggregated data to test whether meaningful within-year differences in the response of output to quarterly monetary policy shocks can be observed across sectors of the economy that differ in terms of their labor intensity. If uneven wage setting is indeed responsible for the differential within-year response of output and prices to a monetary shock, then those differential responses should be more pronounced for sectors that are more labor intensive.[2] In addition, I examine whether wage changes tend to lead or lag price changes. (Since the basic mechanism underpinning Olivei and Tenreyro's explanation for their findings is one in which changes in labor costs affect firms' desired prices, we would expect to see wage movements leading price changes.)

I find no evidence that within-year differences in the response of output to monetary shocks are relatively larger in a sector that is more labor intensive. I find evidence that, following a monetary policy shock, changes in prices tend to *lead* changes in wages, and in addition, nominal wages do not respond as much as prices do to monetary policy shocks. Finally, the response of nominal wages to monetary policy shocks that occur in the second half of the year is slow and muted for *several years* after the shock hits. Taken together, these results suggest that something other than uneven wage setting is responsible for the differential within-year effect of monetary policy shocks on prices and output that Olivei and Tenreyro document.

2. Empirical model and data

2.1 Estimation methodology

The empirical analysis in this paper follows Olivei and Tenreyro (2007, 2010) in using a structural VAR model to measure the response of output and prices to a monetary policy shock. In contrast to standard specifications, however, Olivei and Tenreyro allow the

---

[2] This result could fail to hold if there were systematic cross-sectoral differences in the amount of intrinsic wage rigidity, the degree of synchronization in wage-setting, or both. I have been unable to find any studies that show significant variations in wage rigidity or the timing of wage adjustments across sectors.

effect of these shocks to vary depending on the quarter of the year in which shocks occur. Hence, the reduced-form VAR that they consider takes the following form:

$$\begin{pmatrix} \mathbf{Y}_t \\ m_t \end{pmatrix} = \mathbf{C}(L, q_t) \begin{pmatrix} \mathbf{Y}_{t-1} \\ m_{t-1} \end{pmatrix} + \begin{pmatrix} v_t^Y \\ v_t^m \end{pmatrix}, \qquad (1)$$

where the boldface letters are vectors or matrices of coefficients or variables. $\mathbf{Y}_t$ is a vector of non-policy variables, while m_t denotes the policy variable (in this case the federal funds rate). $\mathbf{C}(L, q_t)$ is a lag matrix of coefficients that allows coefficients at each lag to differ for each quarter of the year.[3]

The assumption used to identify monetary policy shocks is that policy shocks have no contemporaneous effect on macroeconomic variables such as production, employment, and prices.[4] As the analysis here focuses exclusively on the effect of policy shocks, the causal ordering within the $\mathbf{Y}_t$ vector is irrelevant. The impulse responses to changes in the monetary policy shock—v_t—show the effect of the policy innovations on the macro variables. As is standard, the series for the monetary policy shock is estimated using a Cholesky decomposition of the covariance matrix of the reduced-form residuals.

For each variable in the VARs there will be a set of four impulse responses, one for each quarter. It is then important to evaluate whether the quarter-by-quarter impulse responses for the variables of interest are significantly different from the single impulse response obtained from a VAR with no time dependence. Following Olivei and Tenreyro (2007), I assess this with a D- statistic, defined as follows:[5]

$$D_q = \sup_k | x_k^q - x_k | \quad for \quad q = 1, 2, 3, 4 \qquad (2)$$

---

[3] For more details see Olivei and Tenreyro (2007), pp 638-639.
[4] Christiano, Eichenbaum, and Evans (1999) refer to this assumption as the "recursiveness assumption."
[5] The D-statistic is preferred to an F-test because the impulse responses are nonlinear combinations of the coefficients in the individual equations. Thus, an F-test on the linear VAR could indicate seasonal dependence but not necessarily different impulse responses (see the discussion in Olivei and Tenreyro (2007).

This statistic measures the maximum absolute difference between the time-dependent impulse responses of variable x at time k and its non-time-dependent response at time k. The maximum is computed over 16 quarters following the monetary policy shock. Four D-statistic values—one for each quarter—are calculated for each variable. Then, using a bootstrap procedure, a distribution for the D-statistic is computed; the p-values reported for each D-statistic are the percentage of simulated D values that exceed the observed value.[6]

In addition, following Olivei and Tenreyro (2010) I compute the absolute value of the cumulative difference (CD) between the time-dependent impulse responses and the non-time-dependent impulse response for each variable. This statistic captures both the size *and* the persistence of the difference in the responses from the two VAR specifications. Again, this cumulative difference is computed over the 16 quarters following the policy shock:

$$CD_q = |\sum_{t=1}^{16}(x_k^q - x_k)| \quad for \quad q=1,2,3,4.$$

For both the C- and CD-statistics, the bootstrap p-values are based on 2,000 simulations.

2.2 Data

In the case of the 4-variable VAR, the non-policy variables are: Real GDP, GDP deflator, and commodity prices. In the two-sector six-variable VAR, the non-policy variables are: Real services output, services deflator, real goods (durable and nondurable) output, goods price deflator, and commodity prices. The dataset used in the estimations of the various VAR specifications contains seasonally adjusted quarterly real GDP and real GDP by product (services and goods), together with each output measure's respective price

---

[6] New datasets are generated using both residuals (with replacement) and coefficients from the estimated VAR with no time dependency. At each draw, time-dependent and non-time-dependent impulse responses are estimated and a new D-statistic is calculated.

indexes.[7] (Because structures are included in overall GDP but not in the goods or services categories, the sectoral measures do not sum up to total GDP.) The data set used covers the period from the first quarter of 1966 to the fourth quarter of 2007; the starting date is the same as the one used in Olivei and Tenreyro but the ending date is 5 years later.[8] In several VAR specifications, prices are replaced by nominal average hourly earnings (AHE) of production workers in the total private, private manufacturing, and private service-providing sectors.[9] The AHE measure is seasonally adjusted. Olivei and Tenreyro (2007) use compensation per hour in the nonfinancial corporate sector (NFC CPH) for some of their analysis. NFC CPH, however, is not available quarterly for the service and goods sectors separately.[10] The above variables are included in the nonpolicy vector; in addition, this vector includes a spot commodity price index obtained from the Commodity Research Bureau (CRB). A commodity price index is often included in VARs in order to resolve the so called "price puzzle" – an increase in the aggregate price level in response to a contractionary monetary policy shock.[11] The level of the federal funds rate is the policy variable in all VAR specifications. All variables, except for the federal funds rate, are expressed as log levels and a deterministic linear time trend is included in each equation of the reduced-form VAR.

3. Empirical Estimates of the Effects of Monetary Policy Shocks

3.1 VAR specification with aggregate data

---

[7] Ideally, I would use disaggregated data by industry; unfortunately, these data series are only available at an annual frequency.

[8] For the United States, FFR is typically assumed to be the instrument used by monetary policymakers. However, the target for the FFR has been essentially zero for over four years (since late 2008) and the Federal Open Market Committee has turned to unconventional monetary policies. For this reason, the data set used in the VAR analysis in this paper stops in 2007.

[9] Average hourly earnings is the only labor compensation measure available for the sectors of interest over the 1966 to 2007 period.

[10] Using total private average hourly earnings in place of NFC CPH produces very similar results for their VAR specification. Neither measure of wages is ideal as both exclude the government sector, which is included in GDP.

[11] Sims (1992) suggested that the price puzzle arises in specifications in which information helpful for forecasting inflation is omitted. It has now become a standard practice to include commodity prices as they are usually considered to contain information about future inflation.

In this section, I start by replicating Olivei and Tenreyro's results using my dataset and estimation period. I then report results from VARs with wage (rather than price) measures, as well as results from six-variable VARs based on disaggregated data. Throughout this paper, the monetary policy shock that I consider is a 25-basis-point decline in the funds rate. In figures 1 through 8, the impulse responses to the FFR innovation are plotted as solid lines. Eighty percent confidence intervals, generated by repeatedly drawing from the asymptotic distribution of the parameters, are plotted as dashed lines.[12]

Figure 1 displays the impulse responses to a monetary policy shock in a four-variable VAR with no time dependence. The top-left panel shows that the output response peaks about 6 quarters after the initial shock and slowly moves down after that. Prices (in this case, the GDP deflator), shown in the top-right panel, react slowly to monetary policy, rising noticeably four to five quarters after the initial shock. Finally, the bottom-right panel shows that the response of the federal funds rate is less persistent than that of output: The impulse response returns to zero in seven to eight quarters, at about the same time that the output response peaks.

Figure 2 shows the estimated impulse responses from a VAR with time dependence. (In a sense, the VAR with time dependence is unrestricted –responses can vary depending on when the shock occurs; in the VAR with no time dependence – all responses are forced to be the same regardless of when the shock occurs within the calendar year.) The response of real output to a monetary policy shock, shown in panel a, varies depending on the quarter in which the shock takes place. When the shock occurs in the first quarter, output starts increasing rapidly, reaching a peak about 7 quarters after the initial shock. This timing is similar to the response from a VAR with no time dependency, though the peak level of the response here is about twice as large. The peak output response to a shock in the second quarter is even larger and is reached much more rapidly. At the same time, the response also dies out much faster. By contrast, the response of real output to

---

[12] See Olivei and Tenreyro (2007) for a discussion of the confidence interval choice.

monetary policy shock that occurs in the third or fourth quarter are rather small and statistically insignificant.

The price responses (shown in panel b) have almost the opposite pattern to the output responses. When the monetary policy shock takes place in the first quarter, prices respond very slowly and initially even decline slightly; over the 16 quarters following the shock, the response is small and statistically insignificant. The response of prices to a shock in the second quarter is also delayed—prices are only statistically significant from zero about a year and a half after the initial shock. In contrast, prices rise more rapidly and reliably when the shock hits in the third or fourth quarters. Figure 3, for completeness, shows the path of the federal funds rate following a policy shock in the unrestricted VAR. As in the restricted version, the policy shock typically exhibits little persistence.

The p-values for the relevant C- and CD-statistics are reported in Table 1. In all of these tests, the null hypothesis is that the impulse responses in the VAR with time dependence (unrestricted VAR) are identical to the impulse response from a VAR whose coefficients are restricted to be the same across quarters. At the 10 percent level, this hypothesis is rejected by the D-statistic for the output response to a second-quarter shock and for the price responses to a third- or fourth-quarter shock. The CD-statistic, which captures both the size *and* persistence of the difference in the responses across the two VAR specifications, indicates quarterly dependence for the impulse responses of output to first- and third-quarter shocks, and for the impulse response of prices to a third- and (marginally) fourth-quarter shock. For example, the D_2–statistic for real output (the maximum absolute difference between the impulse response to a second quarter shock and its non-time dependent response) is about 0.3 percentage point (not shown). The maximum difference is reached in the third quarter after the shock, when the response in the time-dependent VAR is 0.4 percent, whereas the response in the non-time dependent VAR is about 0.1 percent. For comparison—D_1, D_3, and D_4 are all about 0.1 percentage point. For prices, D_3 and D_4 are about 0.3 percentage point, while D_1 and D_2 are about 0.2 percentage point.

Figures 1 and 2, as well as Table 1, essentially replicate the results from Olivei and Tenreyro (2007 and 2010). Based on these results and the anecdotal evidence for uneven wage staggering in the United States, Olivei and Tenreyro conclude that wage rigidity plays an important role in the transmission of monetary policy shocks. In particular, if the shock occurs in the first half of the year, after wages have been presumably set, the effect on output is large while prices change little. In contrast, shocks occurring in the second half of the year have little effect on real output as wages and prices adjust quickly after that and offset the effect of the monetary policy shock.

Figures 3 and 4 report the impulse responses from four-variable VARs with no time dependence in which the GDP deflator is replaced with one of two measures of earnings —either nominal AHE (Figure 4), or nominal NFC CPH (Figure 5). The responses of AHE and NFC CPH to a monetary policy shock are similar though slightly smaller than the response of the GDP deflator shown in Figure 1; the responses of the VAR's three other variables are almost identical. Once the impulse responses are allowed to vary across quarters, however, the pattern of wage responses differs significantly from the pattern of price responses. Figure 6 shows the impulse responses of wages from two separate time-dependent VARs, in which the GDP is replaced with AHE or NFC CPH. The top panel plots the impulse responses of AHE across quarters, while the bottom panel plots the impulse responses of NFC CPH. Unlike the price responses shown in the bottom panel of Figure 2, the responses of both AHE and NFC CPH following third- and fourth-quarter monetary policy shocks are slow and small for some time after the shock. Indeed, both wage measures typically only manifest significant responses to shocks that occur in the first half of the years. At the same time, the shape and size of the real GDP responses (not shown) are unchanged when AHE or NFC CPH are used in place of the GDP deflator. These results are therefore in line with Olivei and Tenreyro's (2007) findings that the effect of monetary policy shocks on real output depends on the timing of the shock, *but* cast doubt on the hypothesis that uneven wage staggering is the reason for the differential output response.

The *p*-values for the relevant *C*- and *CD*-statistics for the time-dependent VAR with AHE are reported in Table 2. In all of these tests, again, the null hypothesis is that the impulse responses in the VAR with time dependence (unrestricted VAR) are identical to the impulse response from a VAR whose coefficients are restricted to be the same across quarters. At the 10 percent level, this hypothesis is rejected by the *D*-statistic for the AHE response to a second-quarter shock only. The *CD*-statistic also indicates quarterly dependence for the second quarter only. The *p*-values for the *C*- and *CD*-statistics for NFC CPH in the time-dependent VAR with NFC CPH, not shown, are all larger than 0.1 and only in the second quarter the *p*-values are somewhat close to the 10 percent level. This is in stark contrast to the *C*- and *CD*-statistics for the prices.

3.2 A two-sector approach

If uneven wage setting is in fact the source of Olivei and Tenreyro's finding that the effects of monetary policy shocks vary conditionally based on the quarter in which the shock hits, then we would expect to observe a relationship between the shocks' differential effects across quarters and differences in sectoral labor intensity. In particular, if a larger fraction of wages are reset toward the end of the year, and if this causes monetary policy shocks to have bigger effects on output in the first half of the year, then the difference between the quarterly response of output to shocks in the first and second halves of the year should be even more pronounced for sectors in which labor costs represent a relatively greater share of overall costs. To test this, I expand the four-variable VAR to a six-variable VAR, in which the services sector—which is relatively more labor-intensive—is split out from the rest of the economy.

Because disaggregated data by industry are only available annually, I focus on two major product types, goods and services, for which output and price data are available at a quarterly frequency. This breakdown still gives me the opportunity to compare two sectors which differ significantly in labor intensity: For the private goods-producing industries the ratio of compensation to overall variable costs is 0.26, while the corresponding figure for the private service-producing industries it is 0.46.[13]

Figure 7 shows the impulse responses from a 6-variable VAR with separate real output and price measures for services and goods. As can be seen from the chart, the responses of goods output and prices to a policy shock are larger than for services. It is likely that the greater interest rate sensitivity of durable goods explains why goods output (which here includes both durable and nondurable goods) responds more than services.[14] Notwithstanding the relative size of the responses, if uneven wage staggering is the source of the different responses to monetary policy shocks *across quarters*, the differences between the time-dependent responses in the services sector should be more pronounced.

Figure 8 plots the time-dependent impulse responses of real services output (panel a) and the services price deflator (panel b) to a 25-basis-point reduction in the federal funds rate; Figure 9 presents corresponding results for the goods sector. Similar to the results for aggregate output (panel a in Figure 2), services output increases notably and significantly in response to a shock that occurs in the first quarter but, unlike aggregate output, the response of services output to a second-quarter shock is small and, surprisingly, even slightly negative. The responses to third- and fourth-quarter shocks are again similar to the corresponding aggregate output response in that they are smaller than the response to a first-quarter shock with a response to a fourth-quarter shock that is not significantly different from a model with no time dependence. The impulse responses of real goods output (upper panel in Figure 9) show a different pattern. Overall the responses are much bigger than the services responses (note the different scale) but three of them are not significantly different from the restricted (no time dependent) responses. Comparing the

---

[13] I calculate labor share (or labor intensity) as compensation of employees divided by the sum of compensation of employees and intermediate inputs (energy, materials, and services), all from the GDP-by-industry accounts. For the purposes of this study, this ratio gives an idea of the importance of wages for variable costs in the goods- and service-producing industries. The average ratios are calculated using annual data from 1997 to 2010, which is the full time period for which the BEA provides consistent data on the composition of gross output by industry.

[14] Erceg and Levin (2006), for example, have documented that durable goods are much more interest-sensitive than the nondurables sector.

p-values for the D-statistic for services and goods in Table 3, shows that, as expected, the null hypothesis that the impulse responses from a VAR with time dependence are identical to the response from a VAR with no time dependence is rejected more strongly for the services sector than for the goods sector. In addition, the CD-statistics corroborate the persistence of the difference between the responses of service output to shocks in the first three quarters and the response from a model with no time dependence. As for the goods sector, according to the D-statistic, the response to the second-quarter shock is the only one that is significantly different from the goods output response derived from a restricted VAR. Thus, it appears that the notable response of aggregate output to a second-quarter shock is driven by the goods sector, while the aggregate response to a first-quarter shock reflects the responses of *both* goods and services. The responses of both sectors are small if the shocks take place in the second half of the year.

By contrast, both services and goods prices (shown in the bottom panels of Figures 7 and 8) behave similarly, with significant and relatively quick increases in response to a third- or fourth-quarter shock, smaller increases following a second-quarter shock, and outright declines in response to a first-quarter shock. For easier comparison, the upper panel of Figure 10 plots the responses of the services prices from models with and without time dependence; the bottom panel of Figure 10 does the same for goods prices. Figure 10 (along with the results in Table 3) reveals that quarter-to-quarter differences in the price responses for the relatively labor-intensive services sector are not more pronounced than those for the goods sector. Rather, the price responses in the two sectors are similar in direction and in magnitude. Indeed, if anything, the absolute cross-quarter differences for the responses of goods prices are slightly bigger, even though wages should in principle matter less for those prices. For both services and goods prices, the largest difference in the quarter-specific impulse response functions arises for the first- and third quarter impulse responses. The ratio between this maximum distance and the size of the response from the restricted VAR is about 6.5 for both price indexes. In addition, the D- and CD-statistics confirm that the differences between the responses from the restricted and unrestricted VAR models are very similar for these two sectors. The fact that price responses to time-dependent shocks for the more labor-intensive sector are very similar to those for the rest of the economy calls into question whether the observed time dependence in output responses is actually being driven by uneven wage staggering.

For completeness, Figure 11 plots impulse responses for wages from a six-variable VAR where the price deflators for services and goods are replaced by average hourly earnings in each of these sectors. The AHE responses are similar across the two sectors. In addition—and unlike for prices—the impulse responses of AHE to time-dependent policy shocks are very similar to the responses from a model with no time-dependence. (Indeed, according to the *D*-statistic, only the response of services AHE to a second-quarter shock is significantly different from a response with no time dependence.) Moreover, while the price responses for both goods and services were relatively fast and large in response to third- and fourth-quarter shocks, wages in both sectors respond particularly slowly and even decline initially to shocks that occur in the second half of the year. These findings cast additional doubt on the hypothesis that unevenly staggered wages are responsible for the time dependence of price and output responses to monetary policy shocks.

Finally, I consider whether price changes tend to lead or lag wage changes following a monetary policy shock. Figure 12 plots the time-dependent impulse responses of prices and wages for the services sector (upper panel) and the goods sector (lower panel). The price and wage responses are taken from two separate six-variable VARs.[15] The price responses are from a VAR that includes: goods and services output and prices, commodity prices, and the federal funds rate. The wage responses are from a VAR in which the price deflators are replaced by average hourly earnings measures for the services and goods sectors. The two panels show that, following a monetary policy shock, changes in prices lead wage changes when the shock occurs in the third or fourth quarters. This is yet another result that casts doubt on Olivei and Tenreyro proposition that wage resetting tilted toward the second half of the year is the reason why wages and therefore prices respond quickly to shocks in the second half of the year. Wages respond faster than prices only in response to a first-quarter shock; this, however, is the only

---

[15] The data time series is not long enough to run a time dependent (unrestricted) VAR with 8 variables.

quarter for which prices decline in response to an expansionary monetary policy shock (i.e. the price puzzle is present). It is not clear what is driving this result.

4. Conclusion and caveats

Olivei and Tenreyro (2007) offer a novel and intuitive explanation for the finding that monetary policy shocks have effects on output and prices that differ according to the quarter in which they occur. Specifically, they argue that wage contracting is mainly done at the end of the calendar year which causes shocks that occur later in the year to have smaller effects on real output. In this paper, I test this explanation using wage data and two sectors that differ in their labor intensity. While I can replicate Olivei and Tenreyro's basic result, I do not find supporting evidence for an explanation based on uneven wage staggering. If uneven wage staggering is what causes shocks that occur at different times of the calendar year to have different effects, then these differences should be more pronounced in sectors that are labor intensive—something I do not find in my data. In addition, I find that in contrast to prices, wage responses to monetary shocks in the second half of the year are particularly slow. This in turn suggests that the lack of a real output response to these shocks is not because wages are more likely to be adjusted at the end of the year.

While I do not find empirical support for the role of uneven wage staggering, I would not conclude that wages and wage staggering are an unimportant determinant of price dynamics. In the aggregate, labor costs represent about two-thirds of firms' total costs of production. And, it is possible that the measures of wages that are available might not necessarily capture the marginal production costs that are most relevant for firms' pricing decisions. For example, the average hourly earnings measure only covers wages (of production workers). CPH, on the other hand, includes all wages and salaries as well as benefits, but the timing of the bonuses and stock options that are included in CPH may not align with the timing of the work they are intended to reward. As a result, further exploration of the effects of monetary policy shocks on wages—including their temporal dependence—and the importance of wage staggering seems warranted.

References

Christiano, Lawrence J., Martin Eichenbaum, and Charles L. Evans. 1999. "Monetary Policy Shocks: What have we Learned and to what End?" In *Handbook of Macroeconomics. Volume 1A*, ed. John B. Taylor and Michael Woodford, 65-148: Handbooks in Economics, vol. 15; Amsterdam; New York and Oxford: Elsevier Science, North-Holland.

Erceg Christopher and Andrew Levin. 2006. "Optimal Monetary Policy with Durable Consumption Goods" *Journal of Monetary Economics*, 53(2006): 1341-1359.

Peter Klenow and Benjamin Malin, 2010. "Microeconomic Evidence on Price-Setting" NBER Working Papers 15826, National Bureau of Economic Research, Inc.

Olivei, Giovanni and Silvana Tenreyro. 2007. "The Timing of Monetary Policy Shocks" *American Economic Review*, 97(3): 636-663.

------. 2010. "Wage-Setting Patterns and Monetary Policy: International Evidence" *Journal of Monetary Economics*, 57(7): 785-802.

Sims, Christopher A. 1980. "Macroeconomics and Reality" *Econometrica*, 48(1): 1-48.

Figure 1. Impulse responses to a 25-basis-point federal funds rate decline, from a four-variable VAR with no time dependence, by quarter[1]

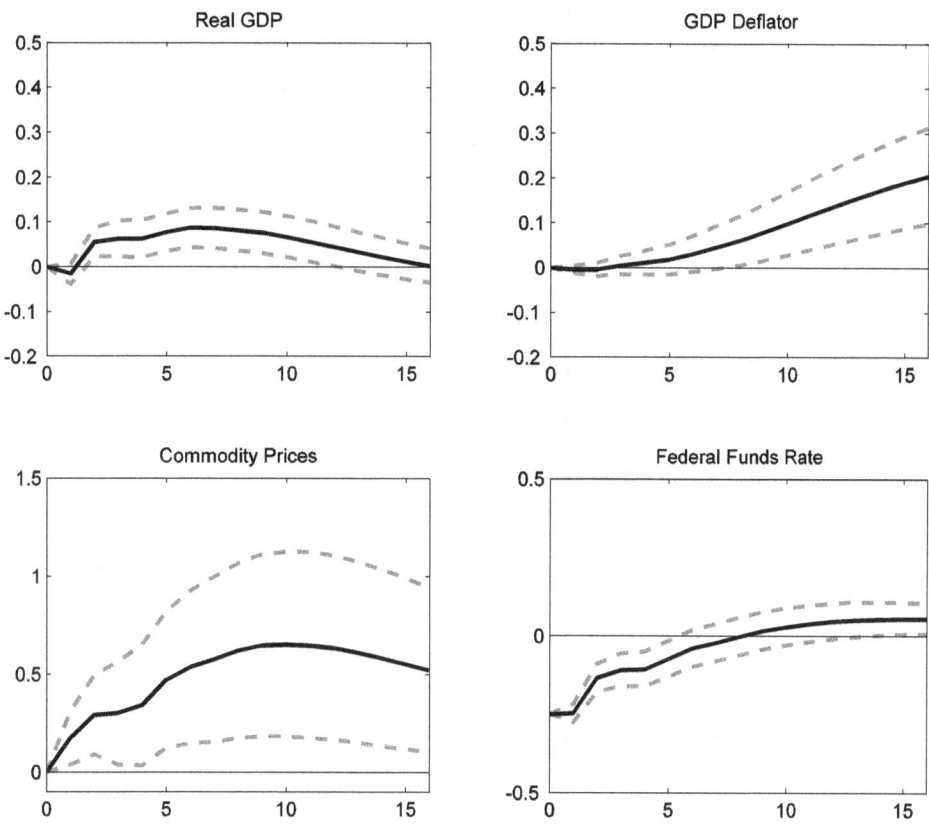

---

[1] In all figures, the vertical axis is in percent and the horizontal axis is in quarters.

Figure 2. Impulse responses to a 25-basis-point federal funds rate decline, from a four-variable VAR with time dependence, by quarter

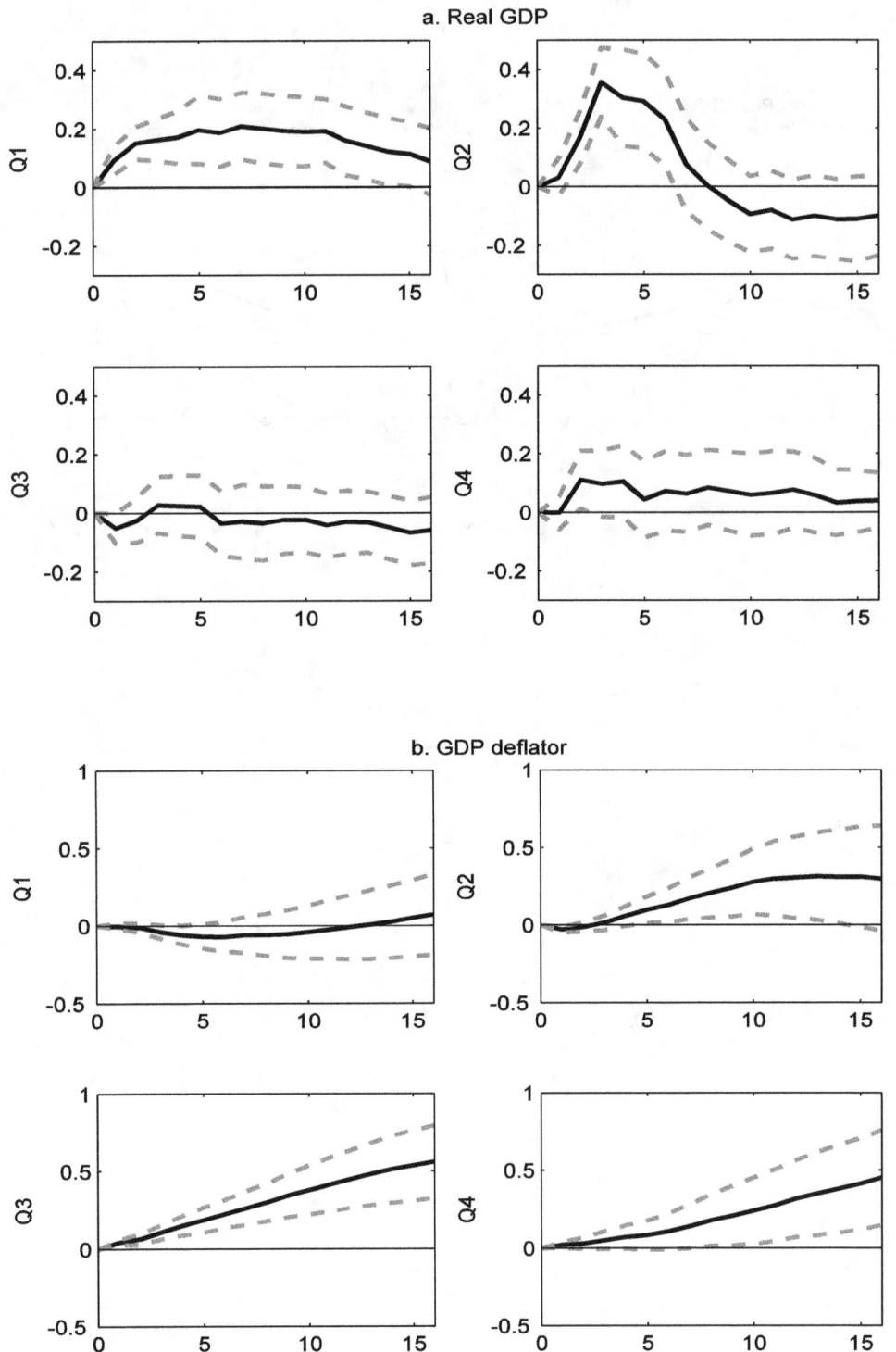

Figure 3. Impulse responses to a 25-basis-point federal funds rate decline, from a four-variable VAR with time dependence, by quarter

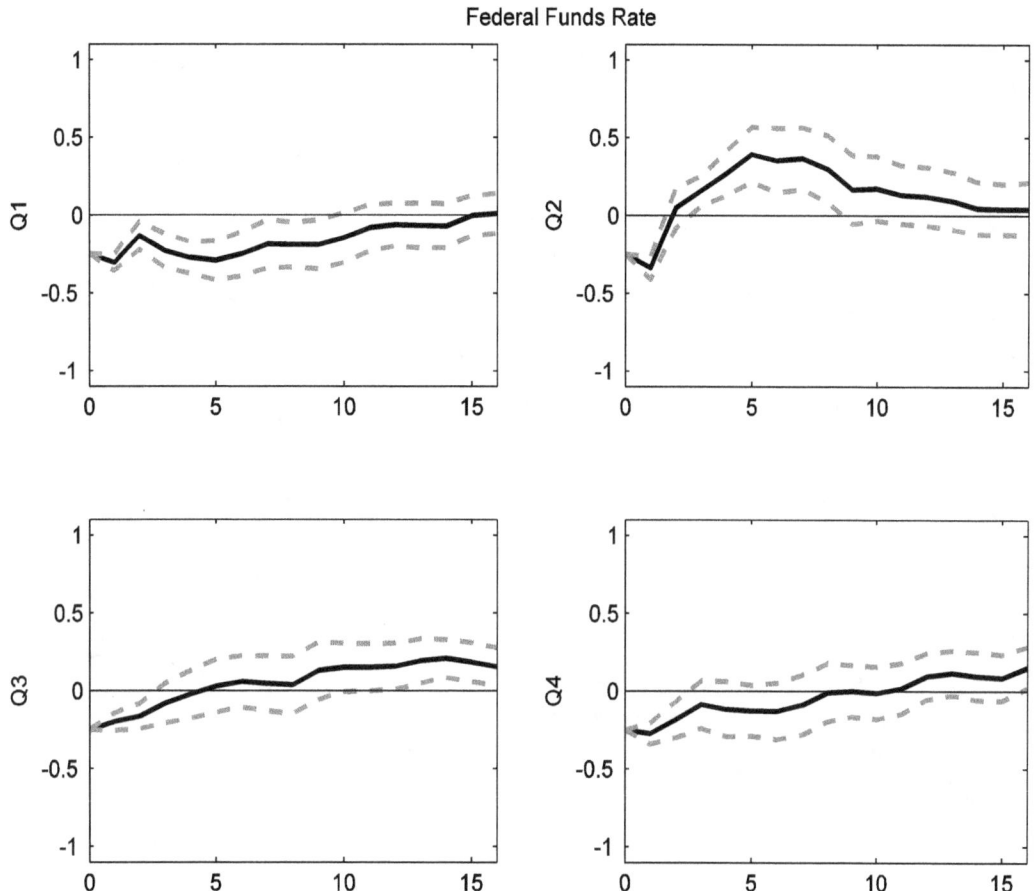

Figure 4. Impulse responses to a 25-basis-point federal funds rate decline, from a four-variable VAR with no time dependence and AHE in place of the GDP deflator, by quarter

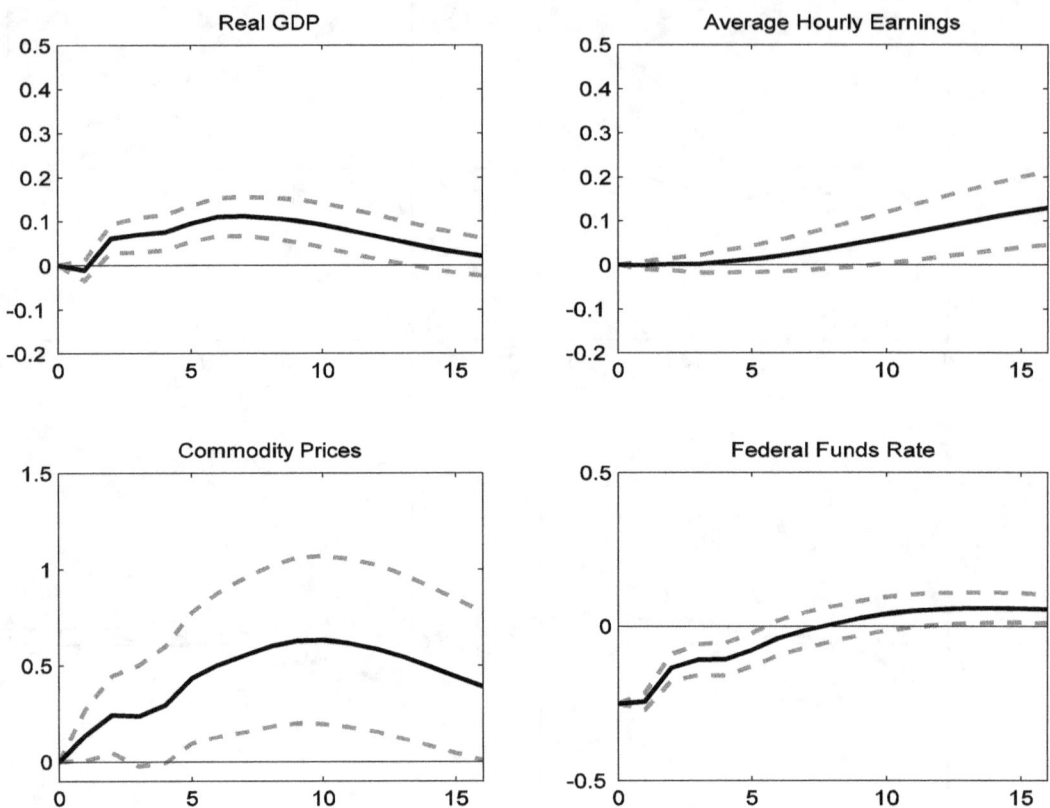

Figure 5. Impulse responses to a 25-basis-point federal funds rate decline, from a four-variable VAR with no time dependence and NFC CPH in place of the GDP deflator, by quarter

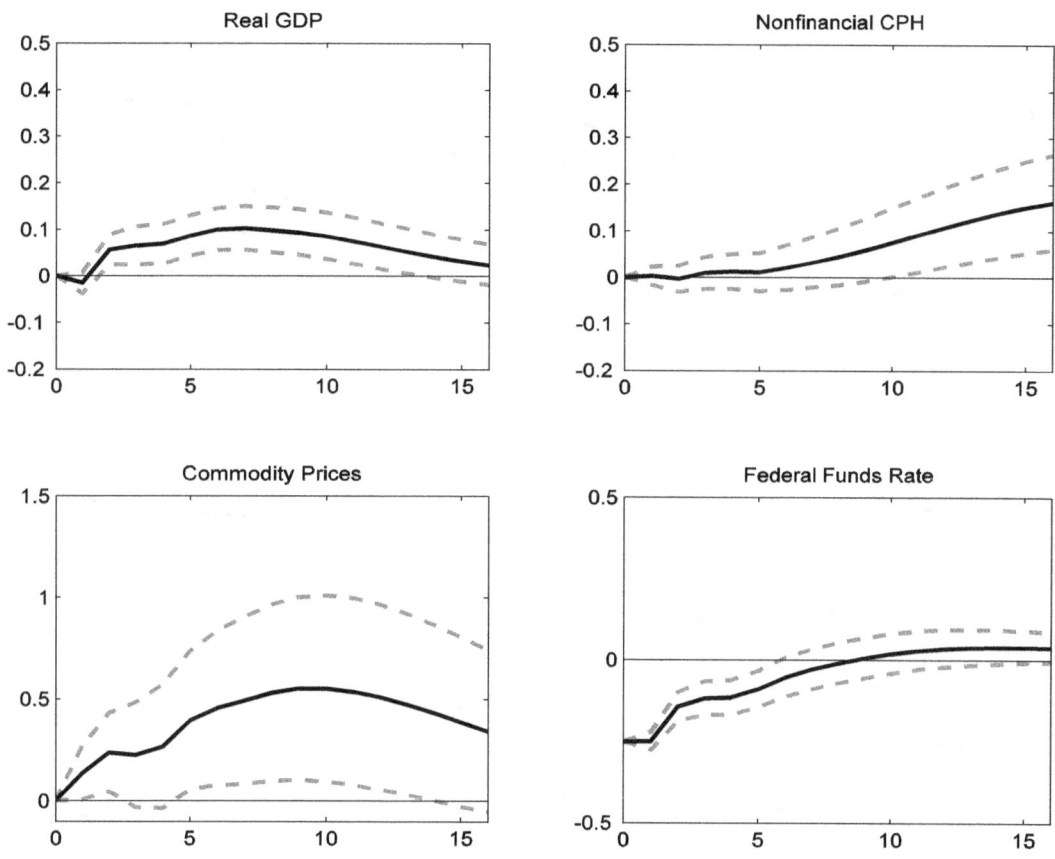

Figure 6. Impulse responses to a 25-basis-point federal funds rate decline, from a four-variable VAR with time dependence and AHE or CPH in place of the GDP deflator, by quarter

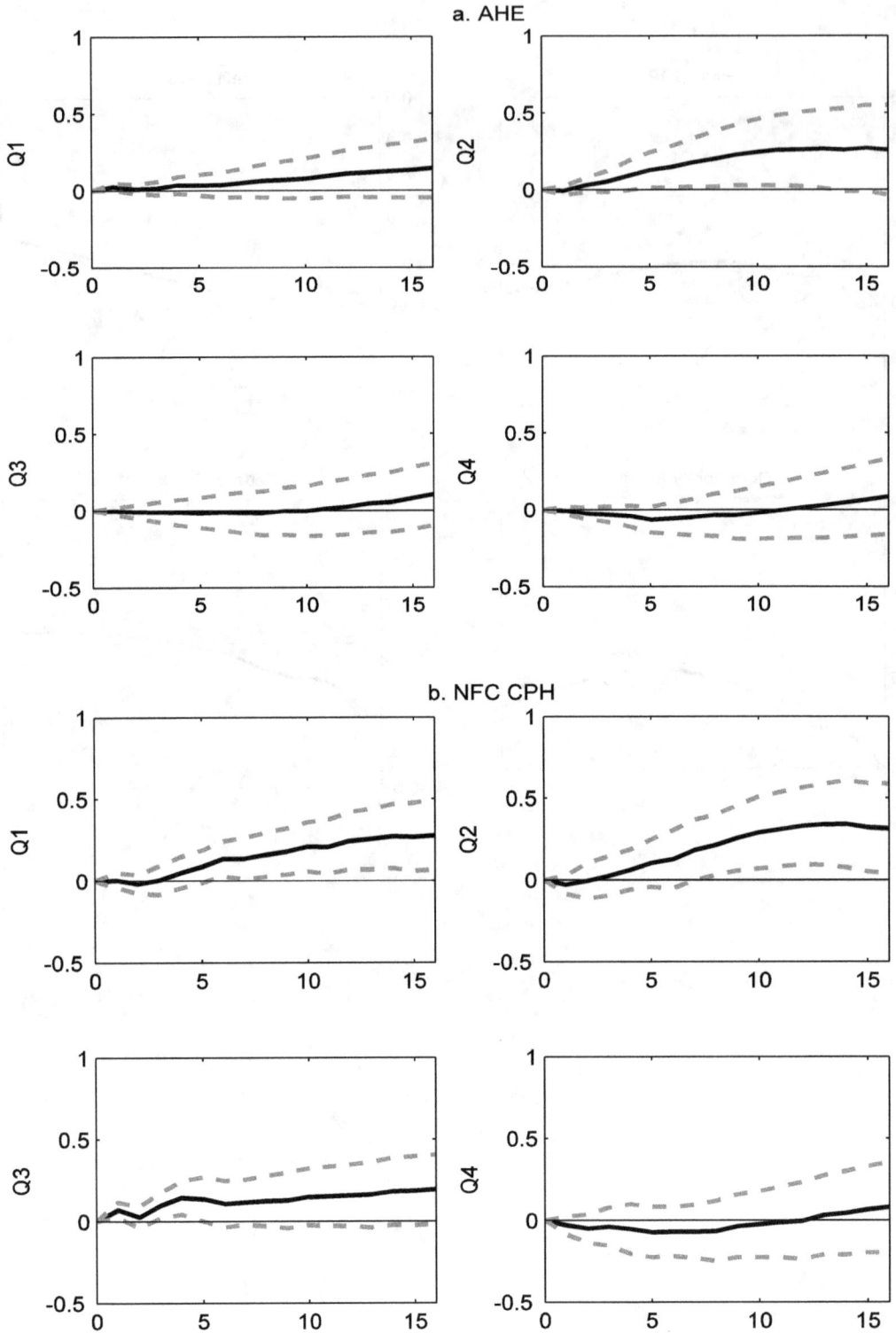

Figure 7. Impulse responses to a 25-basis-point federal funds rate decline, from a six-variable VAR with time no dependence, by quarter

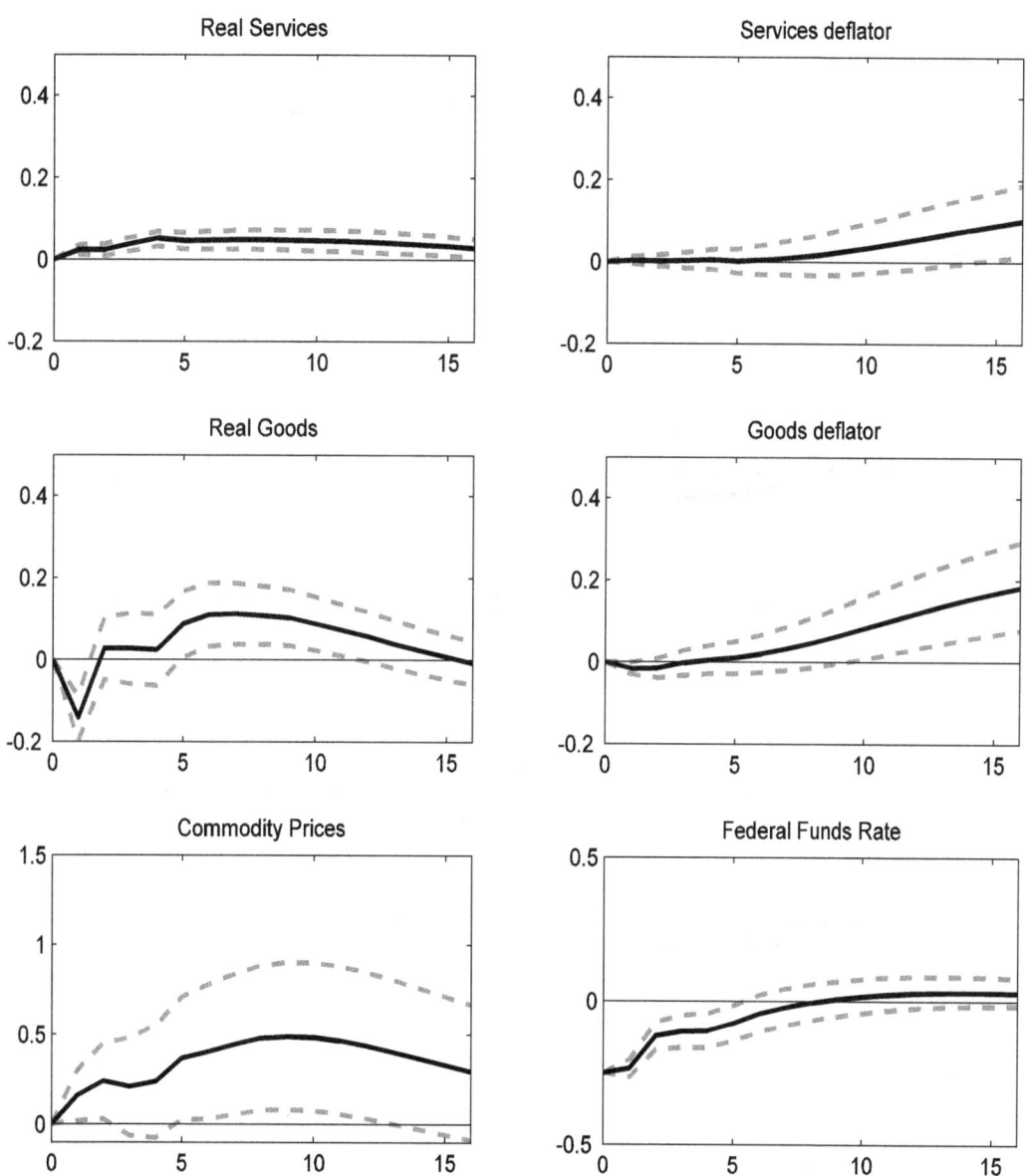

Figure 8. Impulse responses of real services and services deflator to a 25-basis-point federal funds rate decline, from a six-variable VAR with time dependence, by quarter

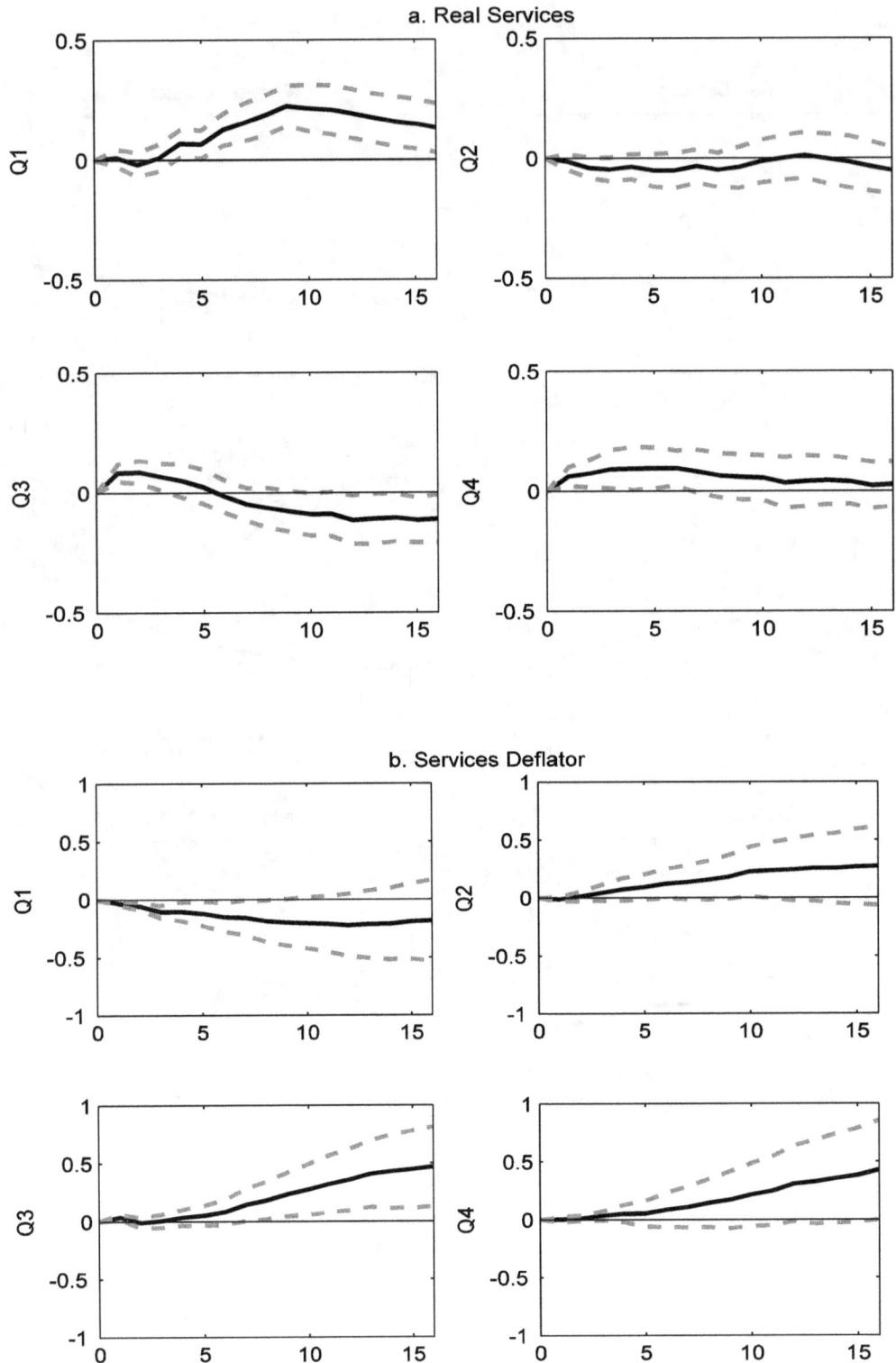

Figure 9. Impulse responses of real goods and goods deflator to a 25-basis-point federal funds rate decline, from a six-variable VAR with time dependence, by quarter

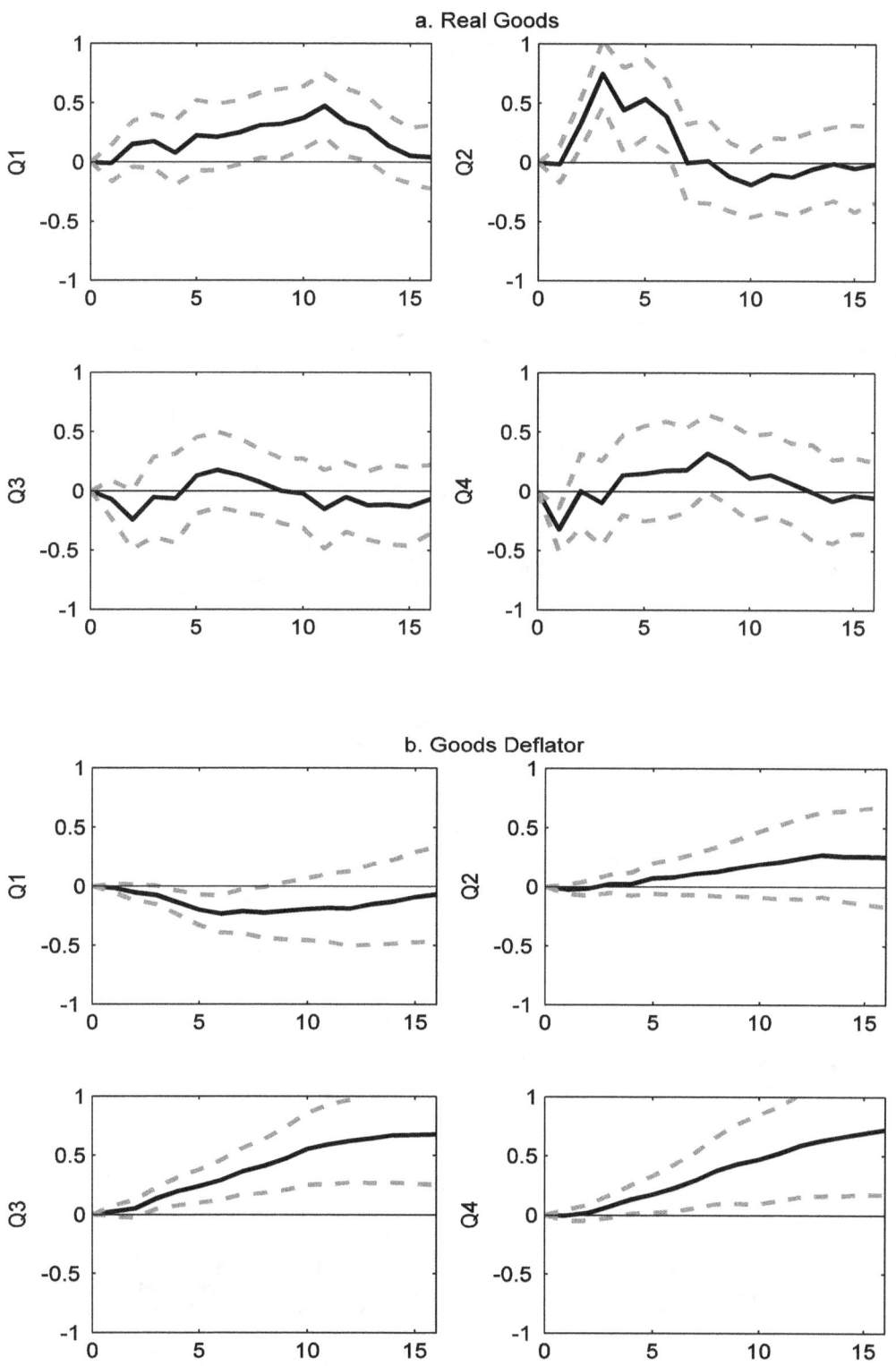

Figure 10. Impulse responses of services and goods prices (deflators) to a 25-basis-point federal funds rate decline, from six-variable VARs with and without time dependence, by quarter

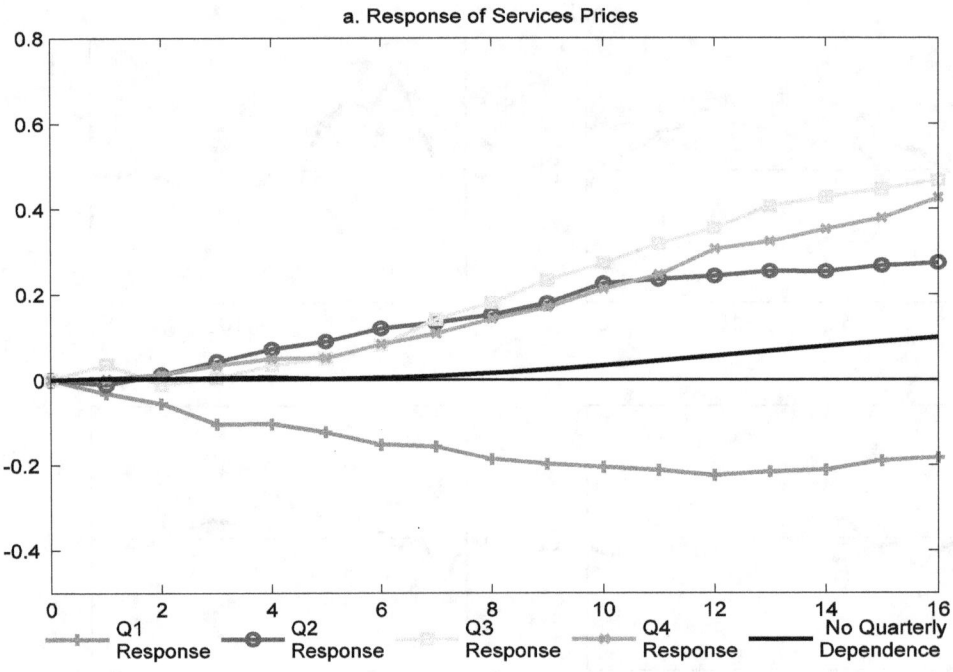

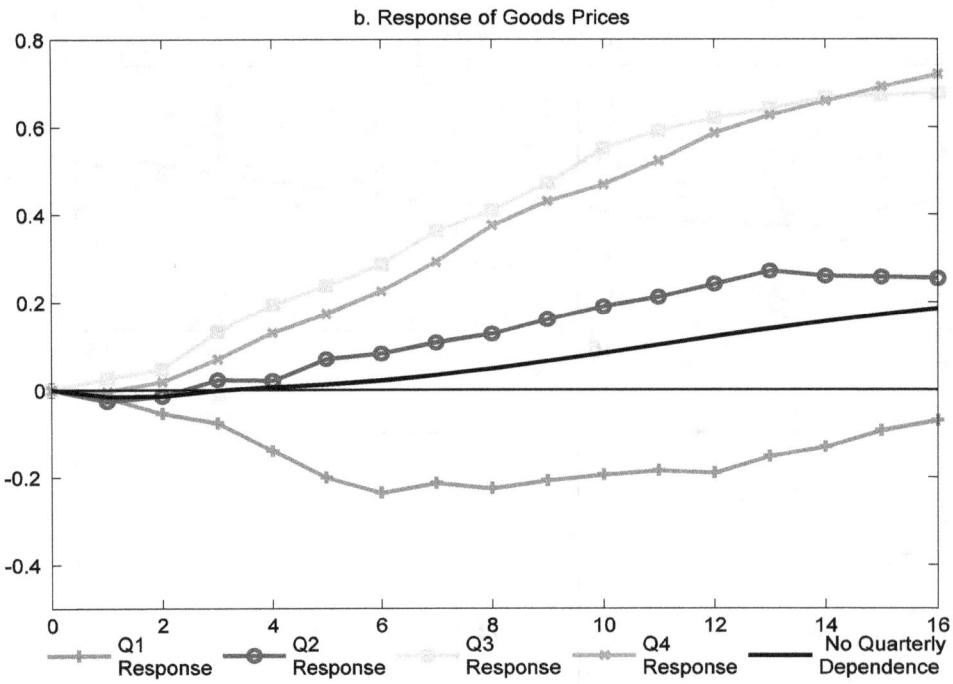

Figure 11. Impulse responses of services and goods wages (AHE) to a 25-basis-point federal funds rate decline, from six-variable VARs with and without time dependence, by quarter

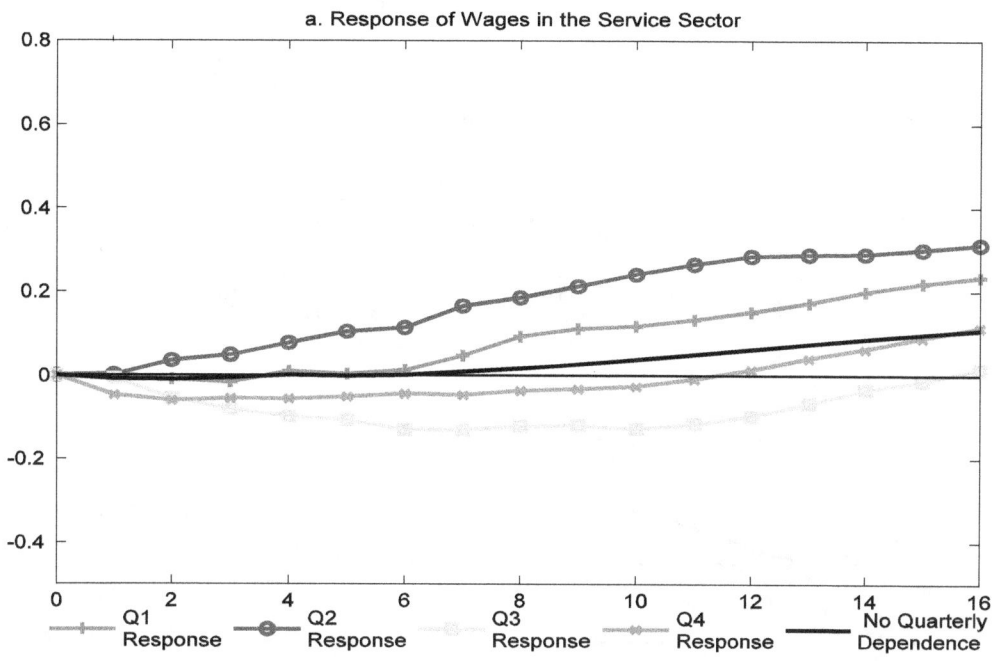

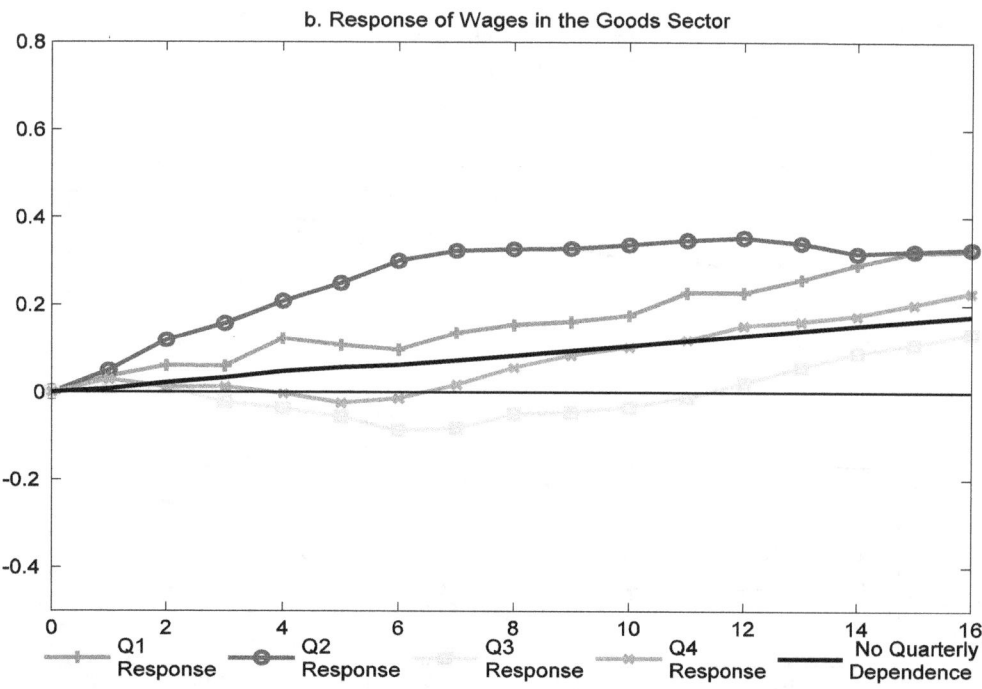

Figure 12. Impulse responses of goods and services prices and sector-specific wages to a 25-basis-point federal funds rate decline, from six-variable VARs with time dependence, by quarter

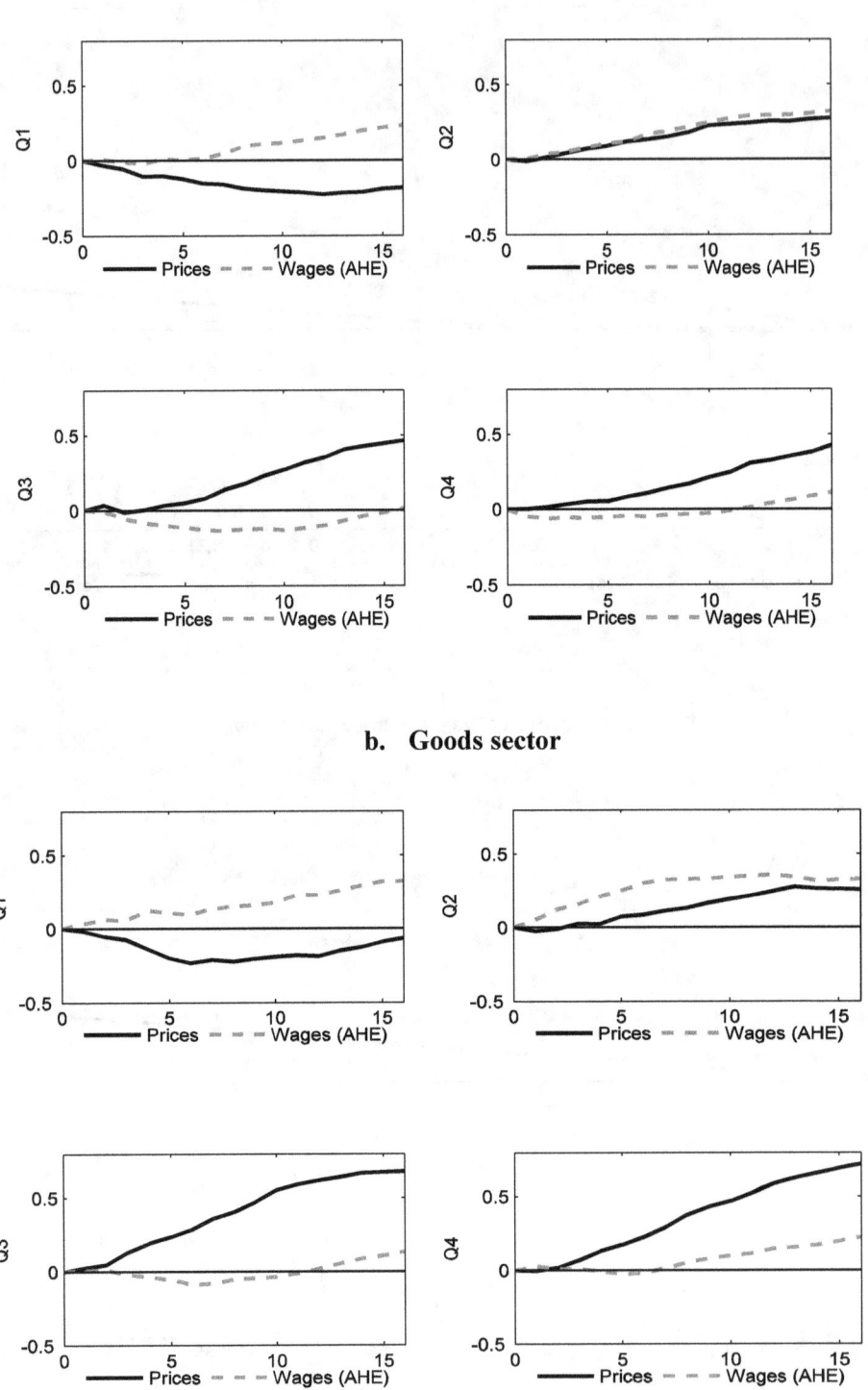

Table 1. Differences in impulse responses across quarters, four-variable VAR (GDP, GDP deflator, commodity prices, federal funds rate)

p-values for the D-statistic	Quarter			
Variable	Q1	Q2	Q3	Q4
GDP	0.23	0.01	0.25	0.83
GDP Deflator	0.28	0.21	0.02	0.09
Federal Funds Rate	0.08	0.00	0.29	0.63

p-values for the CD-statistic	Quarter			
Variable	Q1	Q2	Q3	Q4
GDP	0.01	0.81	0.04	0.71
GDP Deflator	0.19	0.21	0.01	0.13
Federal Funds Rate	0.03	0.01	0.11	0.88

Note: The null hypothesis for both the *D*- and the *CD*-statistics is that the impulse response to a change in the federal funds rate in a particular quarter is identical to the response from a VAR with coefficients that are restricted to be identical across quarters.

Table 2. Differences in impulse responses across quarters, four-variable VAR (GDP, AHE, commodity prices, federal funds rate)

p-values for the D-statistic	Quarter			
Variable	Q1	Q2	Q3	Q4
GDP	0.12	0.01	0.04	0.69
Wages (AHE)	0.90	0.10	0.60	0.43
Federal Funds Rate	0.11	0.00	0.10	0.53

p-values for the CD-statistic	Quarter			
Variable	Q1	Q2	Q3	Q4
GDP	0.01	0.55	0.12	0.66
Wages (AHE)	0.76	0.08	0.56	0.33
Federal Funds Rate	0.08	0.01	0.11	0.33

Note: The null hypothesis for both the *D*- and the *CD*-statistics is that the impulse response to a change in the federal funds rate in a particular quarter is identical to the response from a VAR with coefficients that are restricted to be identical across quarters.

Table 3. Differences in impulse responses across quarters, six-variable VAR (services output, services deflator, goods output, goods deflator, commodity prices, federal funds rate)

p-values for the D-statistic	Quarter			
Variable	Q1	Q2	Q3	Q4
Services	0.01	0.09	0.01	0.52
Services Deflator	0.08	0.23	0.03	0.06
Goods	0.12	0.00	0.38	0.60
Goods Deflator	0.12	0.54	0.02	0.02
Federal Funds Rate	0.06	0.00	0.12	0.45

p-values for the CD-statistic	Quarter			
Variable	Q1	Q2	Q3	Q4
Services	0.02	0.04	0.03	0.49
Services Deflator	0.05	0.16	0.06	0.12
Goods	0.02	0.27	0.20	0.84
Goods Deflator	0.06	0.49	0.01	0.02
Federal Funds Rate	0.08	0.02	0.02	0.69

Note: The null hypothesis for both the *D*- and the *CD*-statistics is that the impulse response to a change in the federal funds rate in a particular quarter is identical to the response from a VAR with coefficients that are restricted to be identical across quarters.

Table 4. Differences in impulse responses across quarters, six-variable VAR (services output, services AHE, goods output, goods AHE, commodity prices, federal funds rate)

p-values for the D-statistic	Quarter			
Variable	Q1	Q2	Q3	Q4
Services	0.08	0.06	0.07	0.77
Services AHE	0.31	0.07	0.17	0.66
Goods	0.06	0.04	0.07	0.61
Goods AHE	0.37	0.15	0.39	0.73
Federal Funds Rate	0.12	0.04	0.25	0.28

p-values for the CD-statistic	Quarter			
Variable	Q1	Q2	Q3	Q4
Services	0.12	0.02	0.30	0.59
Services AHE	0.70	0.06	0.11	0.50
Goods	0.01	0.66	0.06	0.84
Goods AHE	0.38	0.08	0.33	0.92
Federal Funds Rate	0.99	0.01	0.09	0.36

Note: The null hypothesis for both the *D*- and the *CD*-statistics is that the impulse response to a change in the federal funds rate in a particular quarter is identical to the response from a VAR with coefficients that are restricted to be identical across quarters.

www.ingramcontent.com/pod-product-compliance
Lightning Source LLC
Chambersburg PA
CBHW081814170526
45167CB00008B/3437